LET'S-READ-AND-FIND-OUT SCIENCE®

STAGE 2

HOW MOUNTAINS ARE MADE

by Kathleen Weidner Zoehfeld • illustrated by James Graham Hale

HarperCollinsPublishers

Special thanks to Laurence Lipsett for his expert advice.

The *Let's-Read-and-Find-Out Science* book series was originated by Dr. Franklyn M. Branley, Astronomer Emeritus and former Chairman of the American Museum–Hayden Planetarium, and was formerly co-edited by him and Dr. Roma Gans, Professor Emeritus of Childhood Education, Teachers College, Columbia University. Text and illustrations for each of the books in the series are checked for accuracy by an expert in the relevant field. For a complete catalog of Let's-Read-and-Find-Out Science books, write to HarperCollins Children's Books, 10 East 53rd Street, New York, NY 10022.

Library of Congress Cataloging-in-Publication Data
Zoehfeld, Kathleen Weidner.
    How mountains are made / by Kathleen Weidner Zoehfeld ; illustrated by James Graham Hale.
        p.   cm. — (Let's-read-and-find-out science. Stage 2)
    ISBN 0-06-024509-3. — ISBN 0-06-024510-7 (lib. bdg.). — ISBN 0-06-445128-3 (pbk.)
    1. Orogeny—Juvenile literature.   [1. Mountains. 2. Geology.]   I. Hale, James Graham, ill.   II. Title.   III. Series.
QE621.Z64   1995   93-45436
551.8'2—dc20   CIP
                                                                                                                            AC

Typography by Christine Hoffman
11 12 13 14 15 16 17 18 19 20
❖

How Mountains ARE MADE

On Saturdays sometimes we go mountain climbing. We follow a trail through a thick forest.

At first the climb is easy.

Then it gets steeper and steeper. We stop on a rock ledge halfway up and eat our lunch.

When we start out again, we have to walk more slowly. The slope is getting very steep. The forest is thinning out, and the trees are shorter. We can see the top of the mountain, but it seems to take forever to get there.

When we reach the top, we can see out in every direction!
There are hardly any trees up here, and the land is rocky.

We spend a long time looking at the rocks. Here's one with the shape of a seashell in it.

ammonite

Fossils are the remains of animals that lived millions of years ago.

This mountain is more than four thousand feet high. That's nearly a mile. There are no oceans up here. How did a sea animal get to the top of this mountain?

The highest mountain in the world is Mount Everest, in Nepal. It is 29,028 feet high. That's almost five and a half miles. But fossil seashells have been found on Mount Everest, too.

Millions of years ago Mount Everest was not a mountain at all. It was a flat plain under an ocean.

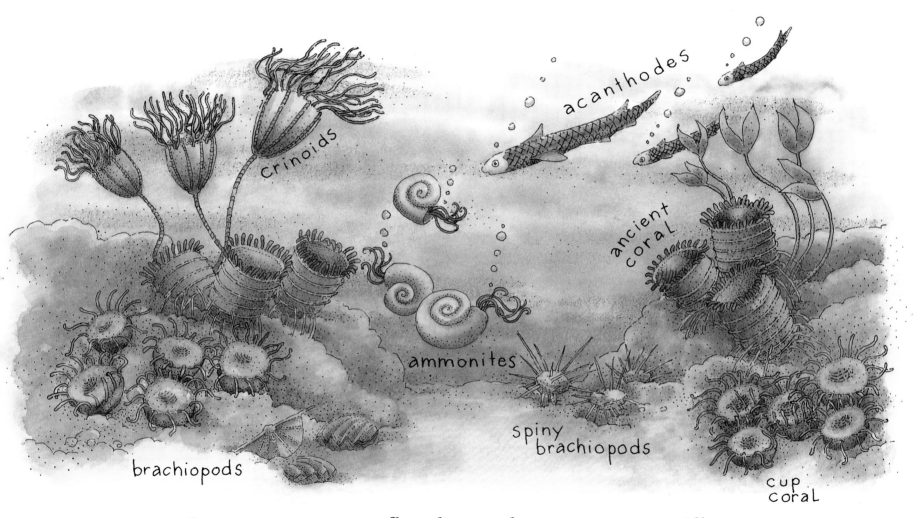

Our mountain was a flat plain under an ocean, too. All sorts of sea animals lived right here. But that was a long, long time ago. Many changes have happened since then.

The earth is always changing. Old mountains disappear.
They are worn away by wind and ice and rain.

New mountains form where there were no mountains before.

We can't see the changes happening, though. Mountains
are built up and worn down gradually, over hundreds of
millions of years.

When we look at the earth, all we see are rocks and soil, and the trees and other plants growing in the soil. But if we could look inside the earth, we would see that it is made up of different layers.

The surface of the earth is the first layer. It is made of the soil and the rocks we see around us all the time.

Just under the surface is a rocky layer, about thirty-five miles thick, called the earth's crust.

Beneath the crust is a layer of solid rock, about sixty miles thick. The crust and this thick rock layer together form an outer shell called the lithosphere.

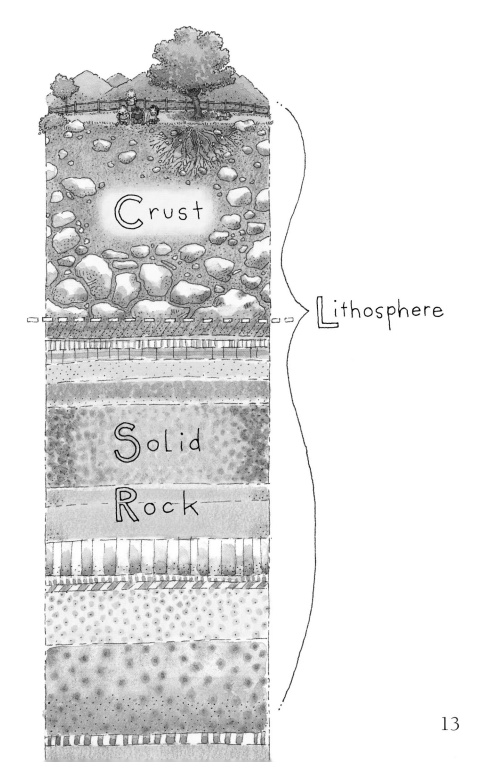

The lithosphere is broken into pieces called plates. The plates are huge. There are eight major plates, and several smaller ones.

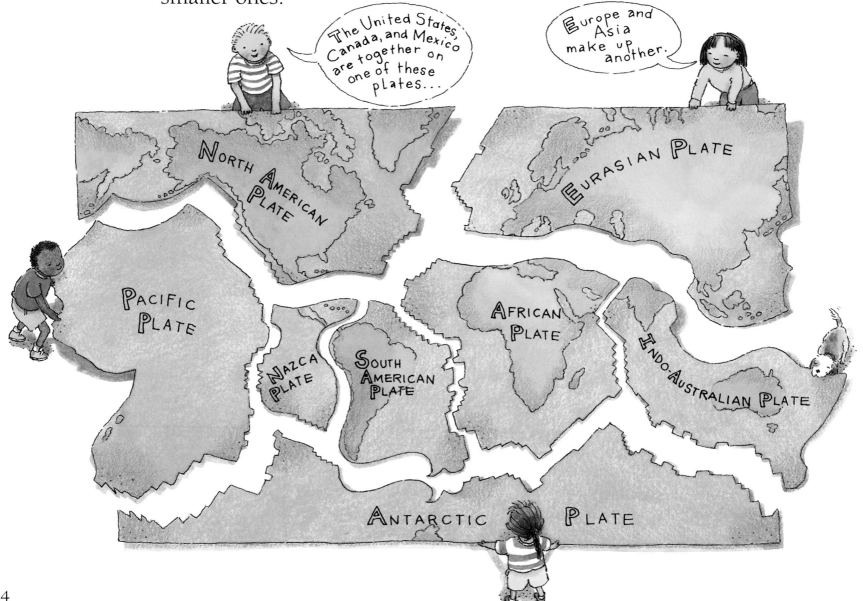

Under the outer shell is a layer of hot, partly melted rock called magma. The rock plates float on top of the hot magma.

The Plates move slowly over the Magma - just a few inches a year.

PLATE

PLATE

CRUST
SOLID ROCK LAYER

LITHOSPHERE

MAGMA

ROCKY MANTLE

The earth's plates are always in motion. They have been moving for hundreds of millions of years.

Most scientists believe that all the mountains on earth were formed by slow movements in the earth's outer shell.

But mountains in different parts of the world look very different from one another.

Folded

Some have sharp, pointy peaks.

Others are more rounded.

Dome

Fault-Block

Still others are block shaped.

A few are shaped like tall cones.

Volcanic

16

That's because in different parts of the earth the outer shell moves in different ways.

In some places two plates press against each other.

The tremendous pressure forces the crust to lift and fold over itself.

Great waves of rock are pushed up. Sharp, craggy mountains are formed.

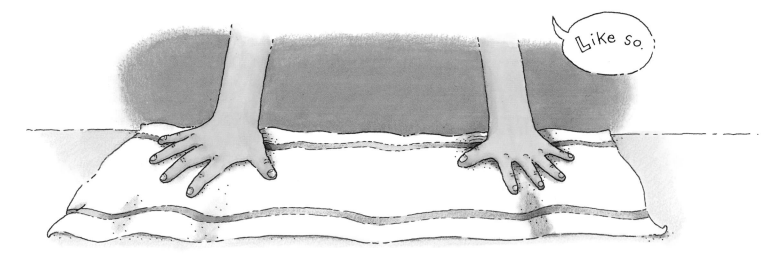

Lay a towel out flat on a table. Put the palms of your hands down, one on each end of the towel.

Then, slowly slide your hands toward each other.

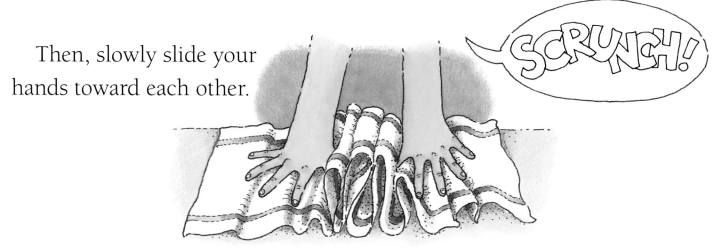

The folds and ridges that appear in the middle of the towel are like the folds and ridges that form giant mountains when two plates press against each other.

In other places, pressure deep within the earth pulls and stretches the crust. The stretching sometimes causes long cracks, or fault lines, to cut through the crust.

Fault-Block Mountains

The crust on one side of a crack may slide slowly upward, while the crust on the other side pushes downward. Block-shaped mountains are formed this way.

Sometimes the crust does not fold or crack. Sometimes magma pushes through a vent in the solid rock layer. It collects in a pocket under the crust.

The pocket of magma grows larger, until it bends the crust upward.

When this happens, a high dome is formed. Rain and wind and ice wash away the softer rocks above, and rounded peaks and valleys appear.

In a few places on earth, plates are moving away from one another. This usually happens deep under the oceans.

When it hits the cool ocean water, the magma becomes solid. Great underwater mountain ranges are built up.

Once in a while a small crack, or vent, forms in the lithosphere—sometimes right in the middle of a plate. Red-hot magma pushes up through the crack.

When it gets to the surface of the earth, the magma cools and hardens.

Once Magma reaches the surface, it's called Lava.

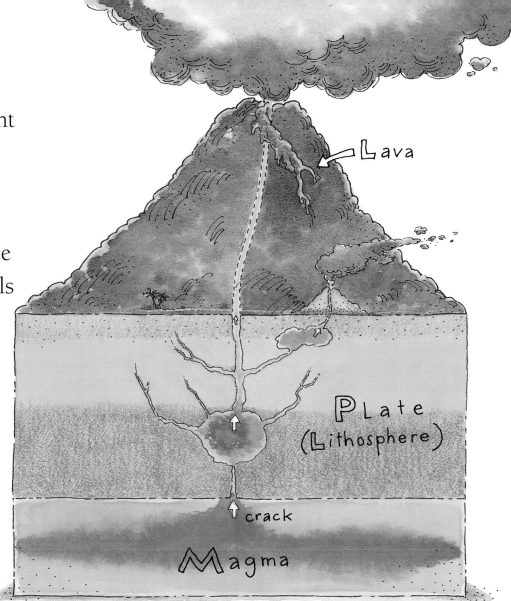

Lava

Plate (Lithosphere)

↑ crack

Magma

Lava and ash build up around the crack, making the land higher and higher. A cone-shaped volcanic mountain is formed.

Most volcanic mountains are formed in places where one plate pushes under another. As the edge of one plate sinks, pressure and friction cause it to heat up.

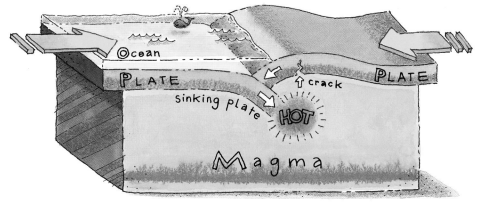

The solid rock of the plate's edge melts in the intense heat. The melted rock, or magma, rushes up through weak places in the crust above.

In fiery blasts, magma is thrown onto the earth's surface. It cools and hardens, and mountains are built.

Some mountains have been around for hundreds of millions of years. Others are still being built up right now.

The mountain we climbed is an old mountain.

The fossil we found can tell us a lot about how old our mountain is.

Scientists have a special way of telling the age of a fossil. This one is nearly 280 million years old.

It died, sank to the bottom, and was buried in sand and mud. It must have been buried sometime just before our mountain began to be born.

25

So, we know that the land here began to rise around 280 million years ago. From the shape of this mountain, we can tell it was formed by a folding of the crust.

Two huge plates slowly pressed against each other. The land rose higher, and the sea disappeared. Over millions of years, the crust folded up in tremendous waves.

This mountain and the other mountains around our town were once much higher than they are now. They were sharp and craggy. Now they are lower and smoother.

For millions of years, rain, wind, and ice have worn our mountains down.

Millions of years from now, the rain, wind, and ice will have worn them down completely.

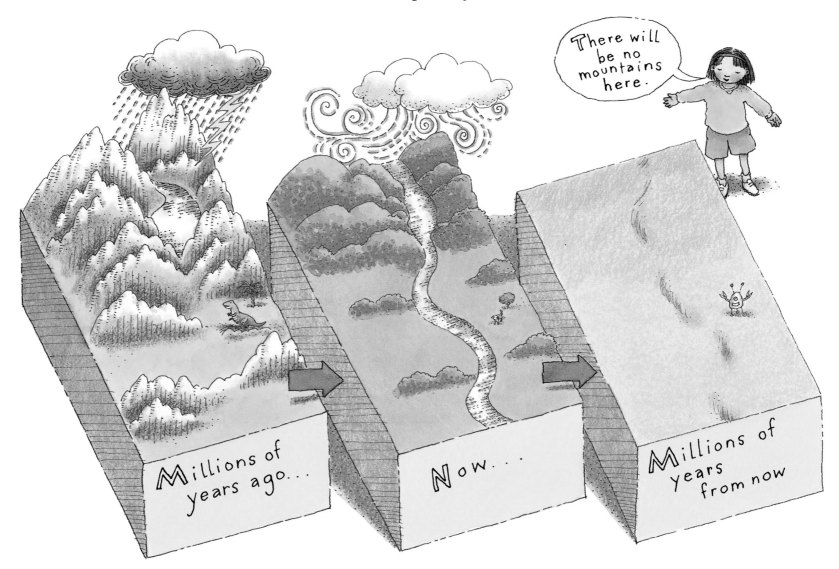

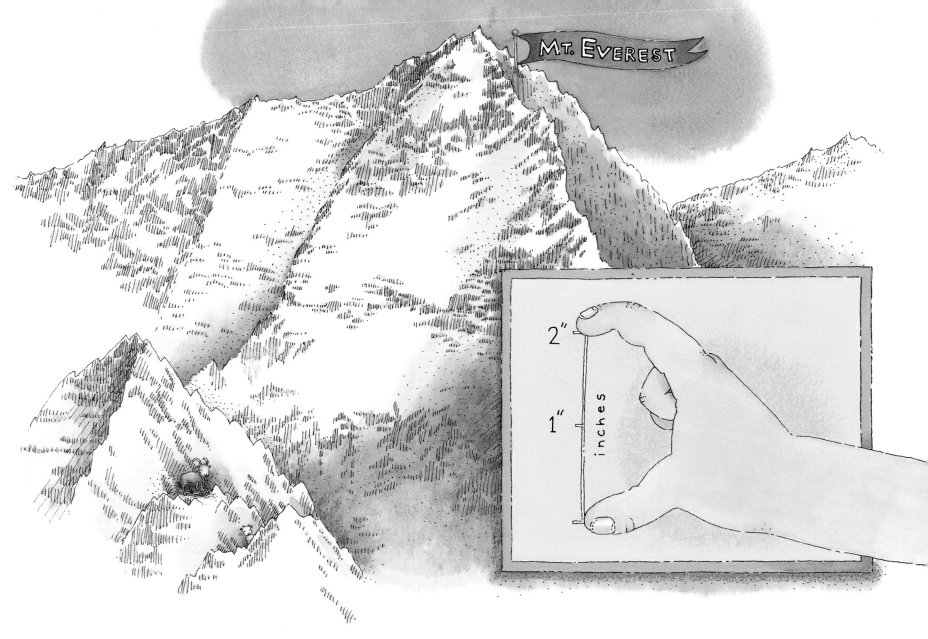

Mount Everest is a younger mountain. It is still sharp and craggy. And it is still being pushed up higher. Mount Everest may be growing as much as two inches each year.